D0687045

NORTH AMERICA'S FIRST PEOPLE

By Janey Levy

Gareth Stevens
PUBLISHING

Please visit our website, www.garethstevens.com. For a free color catalog of all our high-quality books, call toll free 1-800-542-2595 or fax 1-877-542-2596.

Library of Congress Cataloging-in-Publication Data

Names: Levy, Janey.
Title: North America's first people / Janey Levy.
Description: New York : Gareth Stevens Publishing, [2017] | Series: Hidden
  history | Includes index.
Identifiers: LCCN 2016026994| ISBN 9781482457902 (pbk.) | ISBN 9781482457926
  (library bound) | ISBN 9781482457919 (6 pack)
Subjects: LCSH: Indians–Origin–Juvenile literature. |
  Paleo-Indians–Juvenile literature. | North America–Antiquities–Juvenile
  literature.
Classification: LCC E61 .L66 2017 | DDC 970.01–dc23
LC record available at https://lccn.loc.gov/2016026994

First Edition

Published in 2017 by
Gareth Stevens Publishing
111 East 14th Street, Suite 349
New York, NY 10003

Copyright © 2017 Gareth Stevens Publishing

Designer: Katelyn E. Reynolds
Editor: Therese Shea

Photo credits: Cover, pp. 1, 10 Studio - Chase/Science Source/Getty Images;
cover, pp. 1–32 (tear element) Shahril KHMD/Shutterstock.com; cover, pp. 1–32
(background texture) cornflower/Shutterstock.com; cover, pp. 1–32 (background
colored texture) K.NarlochLiberra/Shutterstock.com; cover, pp. 1–32 (photo texture)
DarkBird/Shutterstock.com; cover, pp. 1–32 (notebook paper) Tolga TEZCAN/
Shutterstock.com, p. 5 Mark Hallett Paleoart/Science Source/Getty Images, p. 7
TOM MCHUGH/Science Source/Getty Images; p. 9 Nativestock.com/Marilyn Angel
Wynn/Getty Images; p. 13 Martha Cooper/National Geographic/Getty Images;
p. 15 TUBS/Wikipedia.org; p. 17 Gregory Johnston/Shutterstock.com; p. 19 Clair
Hunt/Buyenlarge/Getty Images; p. 21 Nzeemin/Wikipedia.org; p. 23 John Hyde/
Design Pics/Perspectives/Getty Images; p. 25 World Imaging/Wikipedia.org; p. 27
JENSASTRUP/AFP/Getty Images; p. 28 JEFF PACHOUD/AFP/Getty Images.

Printed in the United States of America

CPSIA compliance information: Batch #CW17GS: For further information contact Gareth Stevens, New York, New York at 1-800-542-2595.

CONTENTS

Words in the glossary appear in **bold** type
the first time they are used in the text.

THE SKELETON IN THE CAVE

In 2007, divers mapping an underwater Mexican cave system discovered something extraordinary. Deep inside, a teenage girl's skeleton rested among the remains of animals from the last **ice age**.

At 12,000 to 13,000 years old, it was the oldest complete human skeleton found in the Americas. And it yielded DNA, which helped solve a long-standing riddle: Why don't the earliest Americans' skulls resemble those of modern Native Americans? Did the two groups migrate from different places or at different times? The DNA showed the ancient Americans were indeed ancestors of modern Native Americans. The dissimilarities weren't the result of different migrations, but simply changes over time.

The chance discovery of the skeleton helped solve one riddle of North America's first people. But the larger puzzle is far from complete because much of the history remains hidden.

REVEALED

The divers who discovered the teenage girl's skeleton named her Naia (NY-uh) after an ancient Greek word for water goddesses.

NAIA'S END

Naia was likely looking for water. The Sac Actun cave system in Mexico's Yucatán Peninsula wasn't underwater when Naia was alive. In fact, the area was quite dry, with no lakes and rivers. Naia and the animals whose remains were found probably entered the caves seeking water and, in the darkness, fell to their death when they stumbled upon the deep chamber the divers named Hoyo Negro, or "Black Hole."

The animals whose remains were found with Naia included extinct creatures such as saber-toothed cats, giant ground sloths, and cave bears.

WHO WERE THE FIRST AMERICANS?

The great questions of **anthropology** include: Who were the earliest Americans? When, how, and from where did they enter and spread across the continent? And what is their relationship to modern Native Americans? Anthropologists and archaeologists develop theories to answer these questions based on the evidence they discover. That evidence is scarce. The earliest Americans had no writing system, so they didn't leave written records. They didn't erect great buildings or monuments. So what evidence exists?

Archaeologists study stone tools and weapons and animal bones. Anthropologists uncover and examine human remains. Genetic scientists study DNA when it can be obtained from human remains. Together, they consider where the evidence was found. They use scientific methods to date it. From this limited evidence, they attempt to uncover the hidden history of North America's first people.

REVEALED

Genetic scientists can also get DNA from coprolites, which are fossilized pieces of poop!

OUT OF AFRICA

Modern humans—*Homo sapiens*—first developed in Africa. All human skeletal remains in the Americas are *Homo sapiens*. More-ancient forms of humans haven't been found. So the peopling of the Americas was clearly part of the spread of modern humans out of Africa. They spread from there across Europe and Asia about 50,000 years ago. They reached what's today Europe about 45,000 years ago. They reached the areas that are today central Asia and Siberia about 40,000 years ago.

It may seem as if there's lots of evidence, but it's all bits and pieces, found buried in the ground at locations scattered across North America. It's challenging to build a meaningful, orderly account from this evidence.

THE CLOVIS CULTURE

In 1932, a road crew working near Clovis, New Mexico, uncovered a pile of big ancient bones. The bones belonged to extinct **mammoths**. Mixed among them were finger-long spearpoints. Quite by accident, the crew had discovered evidence of what was once thought to be North America's first **culture**, named the Clovis culture after the place. The culture appeared more than 13,000 years ago.

The spearpoints, known as Clovis points, are the distinctive **artifacts** of the culture. They're made from fine, easily broken stone and have a lance-shaped tip and often extremely sharp edges. Shallow grooves, called flutes, run from the base toward the tip and may have helped attach the points to spear shafts. In addition to Clovis points, the people also made stone scrapers as well as ivory, antler, and bone tools.

REVEALED

Clovis points have never been found anywhere except North America. They may be the first American invention!

FLINT KNAPPING

How do you turn a stone into a weapon or tool? You do it through flint knapping. The action demands the ability to control how rocks break when struck. The best rocks to work with include flint, chert, jasper, and obsidian. Striking them with another rock or a piece of antler or bone breaks off a piece of rock called a flake. Flakes can be used as simple tools or further worked to create knives or scrapers. The core rock or a large flake can be turned into a spearpoint.

Clovis

Clovis points were made from stones such as jasper, chert, and obsidian. Creating them required time and skill.

Some now think Clovis people hunted mammoths and mastodons so regularly that they likely played a part in the animals' extinction.

No one knows for sure what caused the disappearance of the Clovis culture. It was once suggested a comet crashed to Earth, causing climate changes that killed off ice-age animals and the Clovis culture. However, this has been proven wrong.

Besides its weapons and tools, what else do we know about the Clovis culture? It spread across most of North America. About 1,500 locations have been found. From animal bones found at the sites, we know the people hunted mammoths, mastodons, bison, deer, hares, reptiles, and amphibians. They also gathered plants to eat and may have fished as well.

Beyond that, we know little about them. We don't know what they looked like, how they dressed, or whether they built shelters. We don't know what their society was like. Did they live in family groups? Did they have chiefs or leaders? Did they have individuals whose job was to fight? Did they have religion and priests? This history remains hidden.

CLOVIS FIRST?

It was long believed the people of the Clovis culture were the first to occupy the Americas. The culture was thought to have first appeared about 13,600 years ago. However, recent studies of the evidence using advanced scientific methods have changed the dating. These studies show the culture first appeared between 13,200 and 13,100 years ago and disappeared 12,900 years ago. Meanwhile, other evidence has emerged suggesting humans were in North America before that. The next chapter has more about that.

OREGON'S PAISLEY CAVES

In 2007—the same year divers found Naia's skeleton—archaeologists working in Oregon's Paisley Caves uncovered human coprolites. Fossilized human waste may seem less exciting and important than a skeleton, but the scientists working with the archaeologists were able to get DNA from the coprolites. And what they found changed people's thinking about North America's first people.

The DNA showed some of the coprolites were 14,400 years old. That meant there were people living in and around the Paisley Caves over 1,000 years before the Clovis culture appeared. The DNA also showed that, like Naia, these people were related to modern Native Americans. With the Paisley Caves discoveries, the Clovis culture could no longer be claimed as the first people in North America.

REVEALED
Archaeologists found over 200 coprolites in the Paisley Caves!

MORE FROM PAISLEY CAVES

The people who once occupied the Paisley Caves left behind much more than coprolites. Archaeologists also found bits of rope, mats, and baskets; wooden artifacts; and **projectile** points. The projectile points differ from Clovis points; they're narrower and lack flutes. In addition, archaeologists discovered **hearths** and the bones of animals such as waterfowl, fish, bison, horses, and mastodons. They even found bones of camels, which once roamed western North America!

To most people, this just looks like a chunk of dried mud. It takes the experienced eye of an archaeologist to recognize it's a coprolite that can reveal important information about the past.

OTHER PRE-CLOVIS PEOPLE?

Besides the finds in Oregon's Paisley Caves, discoveries at several other sites have been claimed as evidence of people in North America before the Clovis culture. Some archaeologists and anthropologists believe they've found proof of people in Wisconsin, Pennsylvania, and Florida 14,000 to 16,000 years ago and in Kansas and Virginia about 20,000 years ago. There have even been claims for people in South Carolina 50,000 years ago!

However, not everyone is convinced the "evidence" from these locations can be trusted. It's not always easy to tell what's the work of humans. Natural processes can create rock fragments, or pieces, that resemble broken bits of man-made tools and weapons. Predators can leave marks on animal bones that resemble butchering by humans. So these sites continue to be subjects of disagreement and discussion.

REVEALED

Erosion and animal activity may shift artifacts so it's impossible to tell how old they are by how deep they're buried.

MONTE VERDE, CHILE

Another site where archaeologists claim to have found evidence of humans before the Clovis culture is Monte Verde in South America. It lies far south along the coast of modern-day Chile. There, archaeologists have found stone tools, animal bones, and fire pits 14,500 years old and possibly 19,000 years old! Just as is the case with many of the claims for pre-Clovis sites in North America, however, not everyone is convinced of the evidence and the site's age.

PRE-CLOVIS SITES?

● PAISLEY CAVES, OREGON

SCHAEFER AND HEBIOR SITES, WISCONSIN ●

MEADOWCROFT ROCKSHELTER, PENNSYLVANIA ●

LOVEWELL SITE, KANSAS ●   CACTUS HILL SITE, VIRGINIA ●

TOPPER SITE, SOUTH CAROLINA ●

PAGE-LADSON SITE, FLORIDA ●

This map shows several of the locations where some archaeologists believe they've found evidence of people in North America before the Clovis culture.

KENNEWICK MAN

In 1996, two college students walking along the Columbia River in Kennewick, Washington, stumbled upon a human skull. They called the police, but it proved unnecessary. The skull—and the rest of the skeleton that was found—belonged to a man who died about 9,000 years ago!

Bones yield rich information to those who know how to read them, and scientists learned much about Kennewick Man. He was about 5 feet 7 inches (1.7 m) tall, had well-developed muscles, and weighed about 160 pounds (73 kg). He was right-handed. He was around 40 years old when he died. He had broken ribs that never healed properly as well as other injuries, including a stone spearpoint in his hip bone. Chemical **analysis** of his bones indicated he ate a lot of fish.

REVEALED

Kennewick Man's teeth were worn down to the roots, but had no cavities. That's because—like all people of his time—he had a diet low in cavity-producing sweets.

READING THE BONES

Bones reveal what muscles a person used most because muscles leave a mark where they attach to bones. The more a muscle is used, the stronger the mark is. Kennewick Man's right arm and shoulder resemble a baseball pitcher's, suggesting not only that he was right-handed, but that he commonly made a throwing motion. His knee joints indicate he often squatted on his heels. His leg bones suggest he frequently waded in rapidly running shallow water.

This is a peaceful view of the Columbia River in Kennewick, Washington, where the 9,000-year-old skeleton that's come to be known as Kennewick Man was found.

Kennewick Man's bones also yielded hints about his society. From bone growth around the spearpoint in his hip bone, anthropologists know the injury happened when he was a teenager. They believe he survived only because he lived among people who took care of him. Those same people buried him after he died. Anthropologists know he was buried because his bones show no signs of gnawing or **scavenging** by animals.

Early attempts to get DNA from Kennewick Man's bones failed. So anthropologists used the shape of his skull and bones to try to identify his closest living relatives, which they determined were **Polynesians** and Japan's Ainu people. However, after finally obtaining DNA, scientists discovered Kennewick Man is—like Naia and the people of the Paisley Caves—related to modern Native Americans.

THE BATTLE OVER KENNEWICK MAN

The Army Corps of Engineers manages the land where Kennewick Man was found. When the skeleton was found to be 9,000 years old, the corps ended scientific study and prepared to return it to local Native American groups who planned to rebury it as an ancestor. However, courts ruled the skeleton wasn't related to any living native people and scientists could study it. After the recent DNA findings, however, Kennewick Man will be returned to Native Americans.

The closest DNA match to Kennewick Man came from native peoples of the Northwest Coast, particularly the Colville people. They have long lived along the Columbia River where Kennewick Man was found.

This photo of a mother and child was taken on the Colville Indian Reservation in 1911. The woman may give us some idea of what Kennewick Man might have looked like.

THE BERING LAND BRIDGE

How did the first people get to North America, and where did they come from? The prevailing theory says they crossed the Bering land bridge connecting what's now Siberia, in northern Asia, to modern-day Alaska. Today, the Bering and the Chukchi Seas cover the land bridge. But thousands of years ago, the area was dry land. An ice age had lowered ocean levels by freezing much of Earth's water in massive ice sheets.

Modern humans reached northeastern Siberia about 30,000 years ago. DNA evidence shows these early people, not others who came to the region later, were ancestors of Native Americans. They built settlements such as the one that's been discovered on the Yana River. From there, it wasn't far to the land bridge. But then something happened.

REVEALED

The Bering land bridge theory was first proposed by Spanish priest José de Acosta in 1590!

SIBERIA'S YANA RHS SITE

The oldest archaeological site in northeastern Siberia is called the Yana RHS site. At about 30,000 years old, it's twice as old as other known sites in the region. It's on the Yana River in Siberia's harsh Arctic region. Archaeologists have found stone tools, hunting equipment and sewing tools made of bone and ivory, and remains of animals such as reindeer, bison, and horses. They've also found decorated artifacts and objects meant to be worn as personal ornaments.

SIBERIA

CHUKCHI SEA

● BERING LAND BRIDGE

ALASKA

BERING SEA

Today, the waters of the Bering Strait separate Siberia and Alaska. At its narrowest point, the strait is about 53 miles (85 km) wide.

About 25,000 years ago, Earth got colder and the ice sheets spread further south, pushing Native Americans' ancestors out of northeastern Siberia. But they hadn't yet reached North America. They wouldn't arrive for about 10,000 years. Where were they?

One **hypothesis** is that they lived on the Bering land bridge. It's based on the fact there are mutations, or changes, in the DNA of almost all Native Americans that don't appear in the existing remains of their Siberian ancestors. That means there had to be a population of ancestors cut off from the rest for thousands of years where these mutations could occur. It needed to be a place with animals to hunt and wood for fires. And it needed to be close to North America. The Bering land bridge was such a place.

HABITAT OF THE BERING LAND BRIDGE

Scientists have studied what the Bering land bridge was like at the time ancestors of modern Native Americans might have lived there. It was shrub **tundra**, dominated by dwarf shrubs such as willow and birch. Spruce trees might have grown in some protected places. It wasn't the type of place where you would have found woolly mammoths or bison. But it would have supported animals such as elk, bighorn sheep, and small mammals.

REVEALED

The word "bridge" makes it sound as if the land area between Siberia and Alaska was narrow. However, it was about 600 miles (965 km) wide!

This view of a modern tundra gives some idea of what the Bering land bridge might have looked like 25,000 years ago.

ACROSS THE ATLANTIC?

A few archaeologists have proposed a completely different hypothesis for the origin of North America's first people. They believe people belonging to the Solutrean (suh-LOO-tree-uhn) culture of Europe crossed the Atlantic Ocean to become the first people in North America. These archaeologists base their theory on similarities between stone tools produced by the Solutrean and Clovis cultures.

How did people of the Solutrean culture get to North America? According to the theory, the great ice sheets of the last ice age had forced them to Europe's Atlantic coast. They traveled north up the coast, then around the North Atlantic Ocean, taking advantage of the ice bridge that would have connected Europe and North America at the time.

Is this explanation likely? Most experts don't think so.

REVEALED

The official name for the Solutrean hypothesis is the North Atlantic Ice Edge Corridor Hypothesis.

OBJECTIONS TO THE SOLUTREAN HYPOTHESIS

Experts have objected that Solutrean and Clovis cultures are more different than similar. Clovis hunters didn't make use of marine resources. Solutrean hunters used shore and river resources. Most importantly, the Solutreans lived 5,000 years before the Clovis people. After the discovery of pre-Clovis sites, supporters of the hypothesis tried to link Solutreans to pre-Clovis people. However, not only did the Solutreans live earlier than the pre-Clovis people, but their stone tools aren't similar.

How much do you think these Solutrean points look like Clovis points?

NEW CLUES?

The search for answers to the questions about North America's first people continues. Discoveries keep being made, especially in the area of DNA.

In 2013, researchers mapped the genome of a Native American ancestor buried in southern Siberia about 24,000 years ago. They were surprised to discover he was European, not Asian! So even though the first people may have crossed the Bering land bridge from Asia, they may have carried European DNA.

Part of what keeps the history of North America's first people hidden is that the evidence often seems **contradictory**. A year after reporting on the European genome, the same expert mapped the genome of a 12,600-year-old infant of the Clovis culture. The infant was found to have descended from ancient Asians. He had no European DNA.

REVEALED
The Clovis infant was buried with 125 ancient artifacts, including antler tools.

AUSTRALIAN ANCESTORS?

A group of researchers published a study in 2015 that examined the DNA of Native American populations in South America and Central America. They discovered Native Americans in Brazil's Amazon region had ancestors from Australasia, the name for Australia and its neighboring islands! How did this happen? No one is sure. One possibility is that there was an Australasian population in northeastern Asia that mixed with Asian populations before they migrated to North America.

Dr. Eske Willerslev, from the University of Copenhagen in Denmark, is the expert who studied the genome of the ancient Siberian and the Clovis culture infant. He specializes in the study of ancient DNA.

27

Even the experts disagree about the evidence, as the contradictory studies show. That's because evidence always has to be interpreted.

Anthropologists, archaeologists, and DNA experts will study these bones and interpret the evidence as best they can. But future discoveries may change the way they view the evidence. Future scientific developments may give researchers new tools with which to gather better evidence, causing interpretations to change.

A pair of contradictory DNA studies in 2015 dealt with the hypothesis that Native Americans' ancestors lived on the Bering land bridge for 10,000 years. One study challenged the hypothesis, saying the evidence showed it wasn't possible. Perhaps the people lived on the land bridge for a short period, but a stay of 10,000 years was impossible. The other study claimed its findings *supported* the hypothesis.

It should be clear by now how difficult it is to uncover the history of North America's first people. There's little evidence to go on—fragments of tools and other artifacts and, if you're lucky, bones. The evidence is truly hidden. It's scattered across the country and buried. Perhaps someday you'll be the one who finds the piece of evidence that finally answers all the questions!

ANOTHER PRE-CLOVIS SITE?

Another 2015 study reported on what's likely a pre-Clovis site near a river crossing in Canada. It's at least 13,300 years old and contains stone artifacts as well as horse and camel bones. Archaeologists believe ancient hunters attacked and butchered seven horses and one camel at the site. The date indicates a time before the Clovis culture. However, the stone artifacts don't provide enough information to identify the people.

GLOSSARY

analysis: the act or process of determining the ingredients that make up a substance

anthropology: the study of humans and their ancestors through time and in relation to physical character, social relations, and culture

artifact: something made by humans in the past

contradictory: involving or having information that disagrees with other information

culture: the beliefs and ways of life of a group of people

hearth: a fire-hardened earth floor upon which ancient humans built fires

hypothesis: a proposed explanation of known facts that must be tested against facts discovered in the future to be proven

ice age: a period during which temperatures fall worldwide and large areas are covered with glaciers

mammoth: an extinct type of elephant of enormous size with long, upcurved tusks and well-developed body hair

Polynesian: someone native to the islands of the central and southern Pacific Ocean

projectile: capable of being hurled or thrown forward

scavenge: to gather and remove from cast-off matter

tundra: cold northern lands that lack forests and have permanently frozen soil below the surface

FOR MORE INFORMATION

BOOKS

Harrison, David L. *Mammoth Bones and Broken Stones: The Mystery of North America's First People*. Honesdale, PA: Boyds Mills Press, 2010.

Mahaney, Ian.
Press, 2016.

Walker, Sally M., and Douglas W. Owsley. *Their Skeletons Speak: Kennewick Man and the Paleoamerican World*. Minneapolis, MN: Carolrhoda Books, 2012.

WEBSITES

Locked Away for Years, Skeleton's Secrets Rewrite Prehistory of North America
news.nationalgeographic.com/news/2014/12/141207-kennewick-man-bones-archaeology-ancient-ngbooktalk/
Read what Kennewick Man's skeleton revealed, and see what he would have looked like in life.

Naia: 12,500-Year-Old Skeleton Sheds Light on First Americans
www.sci-news.com/othersciences/anthropology/science-naia-skeleton-first-americans-01925.html
Find out more about the remarkable discovery of the ice-age skeleton in the cave.

The (Pre)History of Clovis—Early Hunting Groups of the Americas
archaeology.about.com/od/clovispreclovis/qt/clovis_people.htm
Learn more about the Clovis culture and possible reasons for its end.

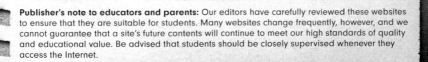

INDEX